A Better Covenant

A Look at the Covenants of God and Our Better Covenant.

Bisi Oladipupo

Springs of life publishing

Copyright © 2023 by Bisi Oladipupo

Springs of life publishing

ISBN: 978-1-915269-26-3 (ePub e-book)

ISBN: 978-1-915269-25-6 (paperback)

All Rights Reserved.

No part of this book may be used or reproduced by any means, graphic, electronic, or mechanical, including photocopying, recording, taping, or by any information storage retrieval system without the written permission of the publisher except in the case of brief quotations embodied in critical articles and reviews.

Printed in the United Kingdom

Unless otherwise indicated, scripture quotations are taken from the New King James Version.

Scripture taken from the New King James Version®. Copyright © 1982 by Thomas Nelson. Used by permission. All rights reserved.

Scripture quotations from The Authorized (King James) Version. Rights in the Authorized Version in the United Kingdom are vested in the Crown. Reproduced by permission of the Crown's patentee, Cambridge University Press.

Scripture quotations marked TPT are from The Passion Translation®. Copyright © 2017, 2018, 2020 by Passion & Fire Ministries, Inc. Used by permission. All rights reserved. The PassionTranslation.com.

Scripture quotations marked (AMP) are taken from the Amplified Bible, Copyright © 2015 by The Lockman Foundation. Used by permission.

Contents

Dedication	IV
Foreword	V
1. Introduction	1
2. The Old Covenants	4
3. What We Can Learn from Old Covenants	24
4. The New Covenant	30
5. How to Implement the Benefits of the New Covenant	48
6. Conclusion	52
About the Author	53
Books Also by Bisi	54
Afterword	56
Salvation Prayer	57

To Jesus Christ my Lord and saviour; to Him alone that laid down His life that l might have life eternal. To Him that lead captivity captive and gave gifts unto men (Ephesians 4; 8). One of those gifts is writing!

Bisi Oladipupo

Foreword

A covenant is a legal agreement, a binding contract.

If you rent an apartment from a landlord, you will usually be given a contract, a legally binding document outlining your responsibilities and the landlord's. Supposing you had a leaking roof and never looked at your contract, you may never know who is responsible for fixing the roof and suffer unnecessarily. To benefit from the contract, you would need to be aware of its contents. This truth applies to our covenant.

In the ordinance of the breaking of bread, we are told that it was the establishment of a New Covenant:

"*In the same manner He also took the cup after supper, saying, 'This cup is the new covenant in My blood. This do, as often as you drink it, in remembrance of Me'*" (1 Corinthians 11:25).

So, we can see that we have a New Covenant. However, we need to know what we have to benefit from it. The New Covenant is also described as a better covenant established upon better promises:

BISI OLADIPUPO

"But now hath he obtained a more excellent ministry, by how much also he is the mediator of a better covenant, which was established upon better promises" (Hebrews 8:6; KJV).

To appreciate what we have, we need to compare it with the covenants in the Old Testament, as our New Covenant is better than the Old Covenant and has better promises.

This book will look briefly at some covenants in the Old Testament and then consider our better covenant.

You will be greatly blessed!

Bisi

Chapter One

Introduction

We can't afford to walk through life not knowing what belongs to us. We do have a better covenant (Hebrews 8:6).

The scriptures say our God is a covenant-keeping God (Deuteronomy 7:9). Have you ever wondered why the Lord fought so much for the children of Israel in the Old Testament? It was because of His covenant with the children of Israel. We will look at this a bit deeper in this book.

When you look at the Old Testament, sometimes, without adequate knowledge, you can easily wonder why God was that way. The simple answer is, it was because of His covenant with His people.

When Moses pleaded for the children of Israel because they were in disobedience, Moses based his prayer on God's covenant with Abraham:

" Then Moses pleaded with [d]the Lord his God, and said: "Lord, why does Your wrath burn hot against Your people whom You have brought

out of the land of Egypt with great power and with a mighty hand? ***12** Why should the Egyptians speak, and say, 'He brought them out to harm them, to kill them in the mountains, and to consume them from the face of the earth'? Turn from Your fierce wrath, and relent from this harm to Your people.* **13 Remember Abraham, Isaac, and Israel, Your servants, to whom You swore by Your own self, and said to them, 'I will multiply your descendants as the stars of heaven; and all this land that I have spoken of I give to your descendants, and they shall inherit it forever.' "14** *So the Lord relented from the harm which He said He would do to His people"* (Exodus 32:11-14;).

It was because Moses reminded God of His covenant that the Lord refrained from destroying the children of Israel.

Have you ever heard someone say begging does not get the job done?

We need to know what we have in Christ. Jesus Christ's sacrifice brought a better covenant established upon better promises (Hebrews 8:6).

If Moses could avert the judgement of the Lord by reminding the Lord of His covenant with His people, how much can we live victorious Christian lives by knowing what belongs to us in Christ?

"For if by the one man's [g]offense death reigned through the one, much more those who receive abundance of grace and of the gift of righteousness will reign in life through the One, Jesus Christ" (Romans 5:17).

The abundance of grace and the gift of righteousness are parts of the New Covenant package.

A BETTER COVENANT

Now, let us look briefly at some covenants in the Old Testament.

Chapter Two

The Old Covenants

The word "covenant" appears more than two hundred times in the Bible. We will not be looking at each covenant, but just a snapshot to highlight the importance and force of a covenant.

When God makes a covenant, you can rest assured that He will always keep His side of the deal because our God keeps covenants (Deuteronomy 7:9).

God's Covenant With Noah and the Human Race

The first time we find the word "covenant" used in the Old Testament is in the Book of Genesis. The Lord had had enough of man that He created, and He wanted to wipe man out (Genesis 6:5-7).

A BETTER COVENANT

However, Noah found grace in the eyes of the Lord (Genesis 6:8), and God established a covenant with Noah. This covenant covered his family and preserved him, his family, and the human race.

*"**17** And behold, I Myself am bringing floodwaters on the earth, to destroy from under heaven all flesh in which is the breath of life; everything that is on the earth shall die. **18** **But I will establish My covenant with you**; and you shall go into the ark—you, your sons, your wife, and your sons' wives with you. **19** And of every living thing of all flesh you shall bring two of every sort into the ark, to keep them alive with you; they shall be male and female. **20** Of the birds after their kind, of animals after their kind, and of every creeping thing of the earth after its kind, two of every kind will come to you to keep them alive. **21** And you shall take for yourself of all food that is eaten, and you shall gather it to yourself; and it shall be food for you and for them"* (Genesis 6:17-21).

This is the power of the covenant. The Lord made Noah create an ark to preserve him, his family, and, eventually, the human race because of the covenant.

So, while the rain was pouring for days and wiping out everything, there was no need for Noah and his family to be concerned because God made a covenant with them.

The Bible tells us that the rain was upon the earth for forty days and forty nights (Genesis 7:12).

Just imagine the kind of discussions in the ark. Imagine the ark rising higher and higher above the earth as the flood prevailed (Genesis

7:17-20). Noah and his family will feel the ark going up and the rain beating on the ark.

Guess what? The only thing they could rely on in that ark was the covenant. Remember that God shut them in (Genesis 17:16), and they could go nowhere. The only thing they could rely on was the covenant that God established with Noah. This is the power of a covenant.

Noah and his family abandoned themselves to the covenant—the covenant that cannot fail. Noah and his family knew they would be saved because of the covenant.

God did the extraordinary to keep His covenant with Noah.

We must remember that Noah did not have a Bible. He did not have any Wi-Fi internet in the ark to check the weather, but only the word of God's covenant.

"My covenant I will not break, Nor alter the word that has gone out of My lips" (Psalm 89:34;).

The next time we find the word "covenant" in the Bible was after Noah, his family, and the animals came out of the ark.

This time, God made a covenant, not just with Noah, but with Noah, his seed, and every living thing. This covenant applies to us up until today.

The Scripture tells us that this is an everlasting covenant:

"⁸ Then God spoke to Noah and to his sons with him, saying: ⁹ "And as for Me, behold, I establish My covenant with you and with your

A BETTER COVENANT

[a]descendants after you, ¹⁰ and with every living creature that is with you: the birds, the cattle, and every beast of the earth with you, of all that go out of the ark, every beast of the earth. ¹¹ Thus I establish My covenant with you: **Never again shall all flesh be cut off by the waters of the flood; never again shall there be a flood to destroy the earth.***"*

¹² And God said: "This is the sign of the covenant which I make between Me and you, and every living creature that is with you, for perpetual generations: ¹³ I set My rainbow in the cloud, and it shall be for the sign of the covenant between Me and the earth. ¹⁴ It shall be, when I bring a cloud over the earth, that the rainbow shall be seen in the cloud; ¹⁵ and I will remember My covenant which is between Me and you and every living creature of all flesh; the waters shall never again become a flood to destroy all flesh. ¹⁶ **The rainbow shall be in the cloud, and I will look on it to remember the everlasting covenant between God and every living creature of all flesh that is on the earth."**
¹⁷ And God said to Noah, "This is the sign of the covenant which I have established between Me and all flesh that is on the earth" (Genesis 9:8-17).

God's covenant with every living creature on the earth is that the Lord will never again cut off all flesh by the waters of a flood. Nevertheless, the Lord went ahead and gave us a sign, which is the rainbow we still see today.

This covenant with all flesh was made many years ago before Jesus Christ even came, yet today, thousands of years later, we still see rainbows.

Our God is a covenant-keeping God.

So, what have we learnt from God's covenant with Noah, his seed, and the human race?

Noah was kept alive with his family because of the covenant. God told Noah to build an ark, and that ark protected him and his family. Our God also made a covenant with the human race that the flood would not wipe out the human race again. He gave us a rainbow, which can still be seen today.

God keeps His covenant.

God's Covenant With Abram

The next time we see the word "covenant" is with Abram.

The Lord told Abram that unto his seed He would give the land, and God mentioned the names of the lands that He would give to Abram's seed (Genesis 15:18).

In the preceding verses, the Lord told Abram what would happen to his seed: that they would be strangers in a land that is not theirs and be afflicted for four hundred years. God further said He would judge the land, and they would come out with great substance (Genesis 15:13-17).

Does this sound familiar?

For emphasis, let us look at the covenant God made with Abram.

*"**18** On the same day the Lord made a covenant with Abram, saying: "To your descendants I have given this land, from the river of Egypt*

to the great river, the River Euphrates— ^{19} the Kenites, the Kenezzites, the Kadmonites, ^{20} the Hittites, the Perizzites, the Rephaim, ^{21} the Amorites, the Canaanites, the Girgashites, and the Jebusites" (Genesis 15:18-21).

Many of us are aware of the mighty signs that brought the children of Israel out of the land of Egypt.

Do you know that God did all those mighty signs through the hands of Moses and Aaron because of His covenant with Abram, whose name was later changed to Abraham (Genesis 17:5-8)?

In the Book of Deuteronomy, we can see very clearly why God brought the children of Israel out of the house of bondage.

"*^{7} The Lord did not set His love on you nor choose you because you were more in number than any other people, for you were the least of all peoples; ^{8} but because the Lord loves you, **and because He would keep the oath which He swore to your fathers,** the Lord has brought you out with a mighty hand, and redeemed you from the house of $^{[c]}$bondage, from the hand of Pharaoh king of Egypt.*

*^{9} "Therefore know that the Lord your God, He is God, the faithful God **who keeps covenant** and mercy for a thousand generations with those who love Him and keep His commandments*" (Deuteronomy 7:7-9).

Here are just a few things that God did for the children of Israel because of His covenant with Abraham.

Remember that Abraham had long gone, as the children of Israel had lived for at least four hundred years in the land of Egypt before these manifestations. This is the power of a covenant with God.

*"Marvelous things He did in the sight of their fathers, In the land of Egypt, in the field of Zoan.**[13]* *He divided the sea and caused them to pass through; And He made the waters stand up like a heap.**[14]* *In the daytime also He led them with the cloud, And all the night with a light of fire.**[15]* *He split the rocks in the wilderness, And gave them drink in abundance like the depths.**[16]* *He also brought streams out of the rock, And caused waters to run down like rivers"* (Psalm 78:12-16).

So, let us have a quick recap of the above verses:

- God did marvellous things in the land of Egypt.
- God divided the sea and caused them to pass through it.
- The waters stood up like a heap.
- God led them by day with a cloud and by night with a fire.
- God split the rocks, and water came out.

Why? All because of the covenant.

Interestingly, the children of Israel were referred to as "servants of God."

"For the children of Israel *are* servants to Me; they *are* My servants whom I brought out of the land of Egypt: I *am* the Lord your God" (Leviticus 25:55).

A BETTER COVENANT

We can also see what the Lord did in another place in the Book of Psalms to keep His covenant with Abraham.

"*He also brought them out with silver and gold, And there was none feeble among His tribes.* **38** *Egypt was glad when they departed, For the fear of them had fallen upon them.* **39** *He spread a cloud for a covering, And fire to give light in the night.* **40** *The people asked, and He brought quail, And satisfied them with the bread of heaven.* **41** *He opened the rock, and water gushed out; It ran in the dry places like a river*" (Psalm 105:37-41).

"*For He remembered His holy promise, And Abraham His servant.* **43** *He brought out His people with joy, His chosen ones with [d]gladness.* **44** *He gave them the lands of the [e]Gentiles, And they inherited the labor of the nations,* **45** *That they might observe His statutes*" (Psalms 105:42-45).

If God, our Father, could go to this length to keep a covenant with His servants, how much more with His children? We are now the sons of God (John 1:12).

While we are still looking at the old covenants, it will be difficult not to compare them with our better covenant.

As the Lord has done so much to deliver His servants, will He not deliver His children?

Further down, the Lord gives in-depth detail about the covenant with Abraham.

"**19** *Then God said: "No, Sarah your wife shall bear you a son, and you shall call* **his name Isaac; I will establish My covenant with him** *for an everlasting covenant, and with his descendants after him.* **²⁰** *And as for Ishmael, I have heard you. Behold, I have blessed him, and will make him fruitful, and will multiply him exceedingly. He shall beget twelve princes, and I will make him a great nation.* **²¹** ***But My covenant I will establish with Isaac, whom Sarah shall bear to you at this set time next year."*** **²²** *Then He finished talking with him, and God went up from Abraham"* (Genesis 17:19-22).

Remember that Sarah was very old at this time.

Now, let us look at the power of the covenant.

What did God do to bring this covenant to pass?

God caused Sarah to conceive in her old age (Genesis 21:1-7). Sarah was at least 90 years old when she had Isaac (Genesis 17:17).

At some point, Abraham took a journey to Gerar and said that Sarah was his sister, and Abimelech, the king of Gerar, took her (Genesis 20:1-2).

Have you ever wondered why God said to Abimelech, "You are a dead man", when he took Sarah (Genesis 20:3)? Remember, it was Abraham who offered Sarah to him. In addition to that, Abimelech could not touch Sarah (Genesis 20:6). Why? It's because of the covenant. The complete account is in Genesis chapter 20.

Let us look at a few of the verses from this chapter.

"And Abraham journeyed from there to the South, and dwelt between Kadesh and Shur, and stayed in Gerar. **²** *Now Abraham said of Sarah*

his wife, "She is my sister." And Abimelech king of Gerar sent and took Sarah.

³ But God came to Abimelech in a dream by night, and said to him, "Indeed you are a dead man because of the woman whom you have taken, for she is [a] a man's wife."

⁴ But Abimelech had not come near her; and he said, "Lord, will You slay a righteous nation also? ⁵ Did he not say to me, 'She is my sister'? And she, even she herself said, 'He is my brother.' In the [b] integrity of my heart and innocence of my hands I have done this."

⁶ And God said to him in a dream, "Yes, I know that you did this in the integrity of your heart. ***For I also withheld you from sinning against Me; therefore I did not let you touch her.*** *⁷ Now therefore, restore the man's wife; for he is a prophet, and he will pray for you and you shall live. But if you do not restore her, know that you shall surely die, you and all who are yours."*

⁸ So Abimelech rose early in the morning, called all his servants, and told all these things in their hearing; and the men were very much afraid" (Genesis 20:1-8).

This incident happened after God had made a covenant with Abraham. Nothing was going to stop it from coming to pass. This is the power of the covenant.

But some said that Abraham lied.

I don't have the answer to that; however, one thing is sure: there was no law then, and sin is not inputted where there is no law (Romans 4:15).

This simply shows the power of a covenant. God supernaturally protected Sarah because of the covenant. She was in Abimelech's house, but he could not touch her (Genesis 20:6). Notice the phrase again in verse 6 : "***For I also withheld you from sinning against Me; therefore I did not let you touch her.***"

In other words, touching Sarah would have been sinning against God. Furthermore, Abimelech and everything he owns would perish if Sarah was not returned to her husband.

Just think about that. That is the power of a covenant with God.

Within the process of time, what God said to Abraham, even before he had Isaac, came to pass. The children of Israel became slaves in the land of Egypt. God remembered the covenant that He made with Abraham. Remember that it took at least four hundred years between God promising Abraham and He remembering His covenant (Genesis 15:13). The Bible says that "God remembered His covenant."

"^{23} *Now it happened after a long time [about forty years] that the king of Egypt died. And the children of Israel (Jacob) groaned and sighed because of the bondage, and they cried out. And their cry for help because of their bondage* [a]*ascended to God.* ^{24} *So God heard their groaning **and God remembered His covenant with Abraham**, Isaac, and Jacob (Israel).* ^{25} *God saw the sons of Israel, and God took notice [of*

them] and was concerned about them [knowing all, understanding all, remembering all] (Exodus 2:23-25; AMP).

When God called and spoke to Moses, it was evident that all the mighty works and miracles that brought out the children of Israel were because of His covenant.

"*Then the Lord said to Moses, "Now you shall see what I will do to Pharaoh. For with a strong hand he will let them go, and with a strong hand he will drive them out of his land."*

*² And God spoke to Moses and said to him: "I am [a]the Lord. ³ I appeared to Abraham, to Isaac, and to Jacob, as God Almighty, but by My name Lord[b] I was not known to them. ⁴ **I have also [c]established My covenant with them, to give them** the land of Canaan, the land of their [d]pilgrimage, in which they were [e]strangers. ⁵ And I have also heard the groaning of the children of Israel whom the Egyptians keep in bondage, and I **have remembered My covenant**"* (Exodus 6:1-5).

God's Covenant With Moses and Israel

After God delivered the children of Israel through Moses and Aaron, He made a covenant with Moses and the children of Israel known as the Ten Commandments. These commandments had to be kept by the children of Israel.

"*²⁷ Then the Lord said to Moses, "Write these words, for according to the tenor of these words I **have made a covenant with you and with Israel**." ²⁸ So he was there with the Lord forty days and forty nights; he neither ate bread nor drank water. **And He wrote on the tablets***

the words of the covenant, the [a]Ten Commandments " (Exodus 34:2-28).

The Book of Deuteronomy, chapter five, also lays out the covenant God made with Moses and Israel.

"*² The Lord our God made a covenant with us in Horeb.*

³ The Lord made not this covenant with our fathers, but with us, even us, who are all of us here alive this day" (Deuteronomy 5:2-3; KJV).

The rest of the chapter lays out the Ten Commandments. There were consequences for Israel not keeping the covenant (Deuteronomy 5:33).

The Book of Leviticus 26 also clearly states that Israel had to keep God's covenant. God also promised Israel that He would not break His covenant with their forefathers in the land of their enemies (Leviticus 26:12-46).

In the New Testament, we have a better covenant established upon better promises.

The Ten Commandments were written on tablets of stone with the finger of God (Deuteronomy 9:10). In the New Covenant, which we will look at later, God puts His laws in our minds and writes them in our hearts (Hebrews 8:10-13).

Isn't it amazing that Moses knew the power of the covenant?

A BETTER COVENANT

The Lord was upset with the children of Israel when they made a molten calf because Moses delayed coming down from the mount (Exodus 32:1-10).

Moses then pleaded with God and reminded the Lord of His covenant.

"*11 Then Moses pleaded with [d]the Lord his God, and said: "Lord, why does Your wrath burn hot against Your people whom You have brought out of the land of Egypt with great power and with a mighty hand? 12 Why should the Egyptians speak, and say, 'He brought them out to harm them, to kill them in the mountains, and to consume them from the face of the earth'? Turn from Your fierce wrath, and relent from this harm to Your people. 13 **Remember Abraham, Isaac, and Israel, Your servants, to whom You swore by Your own self, and said to them, 'I will multiply your descendants as the stars of heaven; and all this land that I have spoken of I give to your descendants, and they shall inherit it forever.'" 14 So the Lord relented from the harm which He said He would do to His people**"* (Exodus 32:11-14;).

Based on that, the Lord repented of the evil that would have happened to the people.

This is the power of the covenant.

After the death of Moses, the people of Israel broke the covenant God made with them. They did not do their part (Judges 2:20). God told them that He would never break His covenant.

"Then the Angel of the Lord came up from Gilgal to Bochim, and said: "I led you up from Egypt and brought you to the land of which I swore to your fathers; and I said, 'I will never break My covenant with you" (Judges 2:1).

The children of Israel subsequently had kings that did not serve the Lord. Yet, the Lord preserved Israel because of His covenant with their fathers.

"*²² And Hazael king of Syria oppressed Israel all the days of Jehoahaz. ²³ But the Lord was gracious to them,* **had compassion on them, and regarded them, because of His covenant with Abraham, Isaac, and Jacob, and would not yet destroy them or cast them from His presence**" (2 Kings 13:22-23).

So, why did God not destroy the children of Israel? Because of God's covenant with their fathers.

Our God keeps covenants.

God's Covenant With David

Solomon was David's son who took over the throne.

When God appeared to Solomon, He reminded Solomon of the covenant He had made with David, his father.

"Then the Lord appeared to Solomon by night, and said to him: "I have heard your prayer, and have chosen this place for Myself as a house of sacrifice.

17 As for you, if you walk before Me as your father David walked, and do according to all that I have commanded you, and if you keep My statutes and My judgments, **18 then I will establish the throne of your kingdom, as I covenanted with David your father, saying, 'You shall not fail *to have* a man as ruler in Israel'** (2 Chronicles 7:12; 17-18;).

When Solomon was praying, we find him reminding God of His covenant with David, his father (2 Chronicles 6:16).

We can see more details about God's covenant with David in the Book of Psalms.

"*I have made a covenant with My chosen,I have sworn to My servant David:*⁴ *'Your seed I will establish forever,And build up your throne to all generations.'* " *Selah* (Psalm 89:3-4)

"*My covenant I will not break,Nor alter the word that has gone out of My lips.*³⁵ *Once I have sworn by My holiness;I will not lie to David:*³⁶ *His seed shall endure forever,And his throne as the sun before Me;*³⁷ *It shall be established forever like the moon,Even like the faithful witness in the sky.*" *Selah* (Psalm 89:34-37).

Could this be why Jesus Christ, our Lord, is identified as the offspring of David (Revelation 22:16)?

It looks like the covenant with David was both natural and spiritual in its implication.

Someone said, "*l wish l could have a covenant with God just like David did.*"

David was secure in his covenant with God. Remember that David was not called a son of God, but we are (1 John 3:2).

Under the New Testament, God has made a covenant with every believer in Christ. This can be found in the Book of Hebrews. You just have to insert your name and personalise it.

"10 For this is the covenant that I will make with the house of Israel after those days, says the Lord: I will put My laws in their mind and write them on their hearts; and I will be their God, and they shall be My people. 11 None of them shall teach his neighbor, and none his brother, saying, 'Know the Lord,' for all shall know Me, from the least of them to the greatest of them. 12 For I will be merciful to their unrighteousness, and their sins [b] and their lawless deeds I will remember no more" (Hebrews 8:10-12).

We need to meditate on this spiritual reality.

We are now the Israel of God (Galatians 6:16).

Could this be why David kept going back to God? Anytime David missed it, he just went straight back to God.

David was confident in his relationship with God and God's covenant with him.

Many of us are aware of what David did. He was not a perfect man, and he did pay a heavy price for what he did in the matter of Bathsheba, but God did not alter His covenant with him.

This is the power of the covenant.

A BETTER COVENANT

Our God indeed is faithful and a covenant-keeping God (Nehemiah 1:5).

When the descendants of David refused to walk in the ways of the Lord, our God still kept the house of David because of His covenant.

"*⁵ Jehoram was thirty-two years old when he became king, and he reigned eight years in Jerusalem. ⁶ And he walked in the way of the kings of Israel, just as the house of Ahab had done, for he had the daughter of Ahab as a wife; and he did evil in the sight of the Lord. ⁷ **Yet the Lord would not destroy the house of David, because of the covenant that He had made with David, and since He had promised to give a lamp to him and to his sons forever**"* (2 Chronicles 21:5-7).

We have to remember that this is long after David has passed on. The covenant was still well and alive and speaking for David.

In the Book of Jeremiah, you see God reaffirming His covenant with David.

"*¹⁹ And the word of the Lord came to Jeremiah, saying, ²⁰ "Thus says the Lord: 'If you can break My covenant with the day and My covenant with the night, so that there will not be day and night in their season, ²¹ then My covenant may also be broken with David My servant, so that he shall not have a son to reign on his throne, and with the Levites, the priests, My ministers. ²² As the host of heaven cannot be numbered, nor the sand of the sea measured, so will I multiply the descendants of David My servant and the Levites who minister to Me.'"* (Jeremiah 33:19-22;).

The Bible tells us that we have a better covenant established upon better promises (Hebrews 8:6), and the Lord is ever mindful of His covenant.

"He has given food to those who fear Him;He will ever be mindful of His covenant" (Psalm 111:5;).

Covenant of the Day and the Covenant of the Night

Did you know that the day and night seasons are a covenant?

Nobody has ever woken up and wondered if the night would not come. We see it as normal, but it is actually a covenant.

Let us look at this from Scripture:

We have already stated part of this scripture, but now we will look at it with another emphasis.

"20 "Thus says the Lord: 'If you can break My covenant with the day and My covenant with the night, so that there will not be day and night in their season, 21 then My covenant may also be broken with David My servant, so that he shall not have a son to reign on his throne, and with the Levites, the priests, My ministers" (Jeremiah 33:20-21; NKJV).

We can see from verse twenty of the above scripture that day and night are a covenant.

A BETTER COVENANT

"*²⁵ "Thus says the Lord:* ***'If My covenant is not with day and night, and if I have not appointed the ordinances of heaven and earth,*** *²⁶ then I will cast away the descendants of Jacob and David My servant, so that I will not take any of his descendants to be rulers over the descendants of Abraham, Isaac, and Jacob. For I will cause their captives to return, and will have mercy on them.'"* (Jeremiah 33:25-26; NKJV).

In light of the above verse, it is safe to say we can find the foundation of this covenant in the Book of Genesis.

"*While the earth remains,Seedtime and harvest,Cold and heat,Winter and summer,And day and nightShall not cease*" (Genesis 8:22; NKJV).

Since we can relate to day and night, it is a good platform we can use to meditate on the power of the covenant.

Now that we have seen the power of covenant in the Old Testament, let us look at lessons we can learn before we look at the new covenant.

Chapter Three

What We Can Learn from Old Covenants

One thing is certain: God keeps His covenant. He does not break them.

From creation (Genesis 8:22), our God established the day and night covenant (Jeremiah 33:20), which still holds fast today. Just think about that.

When Moses was praying for the children of Israel when they sinned against the Lord, Moses reminded God of His covenant (Exodus 32:13), and God repented of the evil He determined to do. Why? Because of His covenant. Moses knew how to pray an effective prayer.

A BETTER COVENANT

The Lord wants us to put Him in remembrance of His word (Isaiah 43:26).

The Lord has also put some things in place so He can remember His covenant, like the rainbow (Genesis 9:11-16).

We enter rest when we know the promises of God (Hebrews 4:11).

In the New Testament, the table of the Lord introduces an ordinance to remember what the Lord did for us and the New Covenant (2 Corinthians 11:23-26). We will look more into this under the "New Covenant." A believer in Christ can use this to remind themselves of the New Covenant.

How did Abraham partake of the covenant that God made with him? He was fully persuaded that what God promised, He was able to perform (Romans 4:21). Note the word used to describe Abraham's attitude. He was not just persuaded but *fully persuaded*.

The Bible also tells us that, against hope, Abraham believed in hope according to that which was spoken that he would be the father of many nations (Romans 4:18).

The Bible also says that after Abraham patiently endured, he obtained the promise (Romans 6:15). Abraham is the father of us all (Romans 4:16); therefore, we can follow his faith.

God is faithful and always keeps His covenant; all we need to do is apply the covenant and align ourselves with it.

Another thing we can learn from the Old Covenant is that although God promised Abraham's seed lands, they still had to fight for them (Joshua 10:8-14; Joshua 10:29-32). It did not just drop on them. When they got into unbelief, they got into trouble (Joshua 5:6). They had their own part to play to fully benefit from what God had promised them.

In the New Covenant, we still fight for what is ours, but our fight is not physical. We fight the "good fight of faith" (1 Timothy 6:12). Why is it called the "good fight of faith"? It's because we have already won.

"Now thanks be unto God, which always causeth us to triumph in Christ, and maketh manifest the savour of his knowledge by us in every place" (2 Corinthians 2:14; KJV).

"Fight the good fight of faith, lay hold on eternal life, to which you were also called and have confessed the good confession in the presence of many witnesses" (1 Timothy 6:12).

Yes, we have a better covenant established upon better promises, which we will look at in another chapter, and we fight the good fight of faith for what is already ours.

In the Old Testament, they had swords to fight with. But under the New Covenant, we have the name above all names, the name of Jesus (Philippians 2:9-11), the word of God, which is the sword of the Spirit (Ephesians 6:17), and the blood of Jesus that speaks better things for us (Hebrews 12:24).

A BETTER COVENANT

We also have the whole armour of God (Ephesians 6:11). In the Old Testament, they did not have this.

The Lord has also given us weapons of warfare that are mighty through God.

"3 For though we walk in the flesh, we do not war after the flesh:

4 (For the weapons of our warfare are not carnal, but mighty through God to the pulling down of strong holds;)

5 Casting down imaginations, and every high thing that exalteth itself against the knowledge of God, and bringing into captivity every thought to the obedience of Christ" (2 Corinthians 10:3-5; KJV).

These are all weapons that will allow us to reap the benefits of our better covenant. The Lord would not give us weapons if we were not in a fight. Unfortunately, we are in a fight, but we have already won because we are only enforcing what is already ours through Christ Jesus.

The Old Testament saints fought with physical weapons, and God backed them up. Likewise, we have spiritual weapons, and they are mighty through God.

Why are things not automatic? Not everything is automatic. For some things, we will have to take our authority in Christ and enforce it.

This is why it is so important that we see ourselves as God's children, because that is who we are (1 John 3:2). We have to rise up, take our authority, and enforce what belongs to us.

Just as God backed them up in the Old Testament in reclaiming what was rightfully theirs, so is the Lord backing us up when we use His name and the weapons He has given to us. The Lord is working with us; the price for our new covenant has already been paid.

The Lord's table, as has been mentioned before, is our introduction to the New Covenant. This will be discussed further later. "This cup is the New Covenant in my Blood" (1 Corinthians 11:25).

The Lord led the children of Israel by hand because of His covenant (Numbers 9:19-23 & Jeremiah 31:32). The Lord wants to lead us into all that Jesus Christ has purchased for us in His own blood. Now, we are led by His Spirit (Romans 8:14).

All that the Lord did for the children of Israel was simply because He loved them and kept His covenant with them.

"7 The Lord did not set His love on you nor choose you because you were more in number than any other people, for you were the least of all peoples; 8 but because the Lord loves you, and because He would keep the oath which He swore to your fathers, the Lord has brought you out with a mighty hand, and redeemed you from the house of [c]bondage, from the hand of Pharaoh king of Egypt.

9 "Therefore know that the Lord your God, He is God, the faithful God who keeps covenant and mercy for a thousand generations with those who love Him and keep His commandments" (Deuteronomy 7:7-9)

The Lord fought for Israel after they left Egypt because of His covenant. The land of the Amorites was part of the land that the Lord made a covenant to give to Abram's seed (Genesis 15:18-21). The Lord told Joshua that He had delivered them into the hands of Israel. The Lord fought for Israel and cast stones from heaven upon them (Joshua 10:8-12).

What we can learn from the Old Covenant is that we each have our own role to play. We must align ourselves and apply spiritual principles to partake of it. We will have a different look under the New Covenant.

Chapter Four

The New Covenant

Now that we have looked at some covenants in the Old Testament, let us consider the New Covenant.

The Lord's table introduces us to the New Covenant. The words "testament" and "covenant" are the same.

When our Lord Jesus Christ introduced the table of the Lord to His disciples, it was clear that this was the introduction to the New Covenant.

"[19] And He took bread, gave thanks and broke it, and gave it to them, saying, "This is My body which is given for you; do this in remembrance of Me."

A BETTER COVENANT

²⁰ Likewise He also took the cup after supper, saying, **"This cup is the new covenant in My blood, which is shed for you"** (Luke 22:19-20).

Paul also confirmed that he had received this ordinance from the Lord:

"²³ For I received from the Lord that which I also delivered to you: that the Lord Jesus on the same night in which He was betrayed took bread; ²⁴ and when He had given thanks, He broke it and said, [d]"Take, eat; this is My body which is [e]broken for you; do this in remembrance of Me." ²⁵ In the same manner He also took the cup after supper, saying, "This cup is the new covenant in My blood. This do, as often as you drink it, in remembrance of Me" (1 Corinthians 11:23-25).

Now, let us look at the phrase, *"This cup is the new covenant in My blood. This do, as often as you drink it, in remembrance of Me."*

Jesus was saying here that the cup represented the price He paid for us all in His blood for the New Covenant. To further explain the "cup" in this verse, I would refer you to read the book, *The Lord's Cup in Communion,* by Bisi Oladipupo.

When we lift up the cup in communion, we remember the suffering of our Lord Jesus Christ and the price He paid for the New Covenant with His own blood.

For just a brief recap, the cup represents the suffering of the Lord. From the account of when Jesus was in Gethsemane, it is clear that the cup represented the suffering and price that He paid for us all.

"³⁶ Then Jesus came with them to a place called Gethsemane, and said to the disciples, "Sit here while I go and pray over there." ³⁷ And He took with Him Peter and the two sons of Zebedee, and He began to be sorrowful and deeply distressed. ³⁸ Then He said to them, "My soul is exceedingly sorrowful, even to death. Stay here and watch with Me."

³⁹ He went a little farther and fell on His face, and prayed, saying, **"O My Father, if it is possible, let this cup pass from Me; nevertheless, not as I will, but as You will"** (Matthew 26:36-39).

As we can see from the above verses, just before the Lord paid the price for us, He asked the Father, **"*if it is possible, let this cup pass from Me.*"** So, what was in the cup? The price Jesus paid for us in His own blood.

Therefore, looking at the New Covenant, it is safe to say that all Jesus suffered for us and took our place for are the benefits of the New Covenant. However, let us also remember that it is a better covenant established on better promises.

The Book of Hebrews also gives us insight into our better covenant.

"⁷ For if that first covenant had been faultless, then no place would have been sought for a second. ⁸ Because finding fault with them, He says: "Behold, the days are coming, says the Lord, when I will make a new covenant with the house of Israel and with the house of Judah— ⁹ not according to the covenant that I made with their fathers in the day when I took them by the hand to lead them out of the land of Egypt; because they did not continue in My covenant, and I disregarded them, says the Lord. ¹⁰ For this is the covenant that I will make with the house of Israel

after those days, says the Lord: I will put My laws in their mind and write them on their hearts; and I will be their God, and they shall be My people. ***11*** *None of them shall teach his neighbor, and none his brother, saying, 'Know the Lord,' for all shall know Me, from the least of them to the greatest of them.* ***12*** *For I will be merciful to their unrighteousness, and their sins [b] and their lawless deeds I will remember no more."*

13 *In that He says, "A new covenant," He has made the first obsolete. Now what is becoming obsolete and growing old is ready to vanish away"* (Hebrews 8:7-13).

We are now called the Israel of God (Galatians 6:16).

"***15*** *Whereof the Holy Ghost also is a witness to us: for after that he had said before,*

16 *This is the covenant that I will make with them after those days, saith the Lord, I will put my laws into their hearts, and in their minds will I write them;*

17 *And their sins and iniquities will I remember no more"* (Hebrews 10:15-17; KJV).

Now that we know how powerful a covenant is and that our God is a covenant-keeping God, let us look further into our New Covenant.

It has already been stated that the cup is Jesus' suffering for us in His blood, which established the New Covenant. Therefore, everything Jesus Christ accomplished for us and the price He paid are our entrance into the New Covenant.

The entrance to becoming a partaker of the New Covenant is to receive and confess Jesus Christ as Lord and Saviour. *For whosoever shall call upon the name of the Lord shall be saved* (Romans 10:13; KJV). Receiving Jesus Christ as Lord and Saviour transfers a person from the power of darkness into the Kingdom of Jesus Christ (Colossians 1:13). The New Covenant operates under the Lordship of Jesus Christ. In Christ, we become partakers of the covenants of promise (Ephesians 2:12).

Now, let us look at our benefits under the New Covenant. Once again, remember that our God keeps covenants. This will give us confidence. It has nothing to do with our fleshly feelings but with the integrity of the word of God and His covenant with us. As believers in Christ, we are now in the Spirit (Romans 8:9).

Dead to Sin

"*Who his own self bare our sins in his own body on the tree, that we, being dead to sins, should live unto righteousness: by whose stripes ye were healed*" (1 Peter 2:24).

Under the New Covenant, we are dead to sin and alive to righteousness. Any struggles we have, we must take it to the Lord in prayer and make a decision that we will live a godly life. We must also renew our minds to accept this reality.

The Bible says that as new born babes, we should desire the sincere milk of the word that we may grow (1 Peter 2:2). The Word of God is also referred to as water (Ephesians 5:26). As we spend time in the

Word of God, it cleanses us. Things that we used to desire will simply begin to drop off.

Our struggles are in the flesh. This is why we have to walk in the Spirit and see ourselves the way God sees us.

We live through Christ (1 John 4:9), so we are not walking this life in our own strength.

Forgiveness of Sins

The sacrifice of Jesus Christ has brought us forgiveness for our sins.

"In whom we have redemption through his blood, even the forgiveness of sins" (Colossians 1:14; KJV).

Have you ever heard someone say they still feel guilty even though they have confessed their sins? This should not be so. *If we confess our sins, He is faithful and just to forgive us our sins, and to cleanse us from all unrighteousness* (1 John 1:9; KJV).

Why is the Lord faithful and just to forgive us our sins? It's not because of us but because of the New Covenant. We are forgiven because of Christ's sake (Ephesians 4:32).

That should give us confidence whenever we ask God to forgive our sins. When we miss it, we simply have to repent, and the Lord will forgive us.

Intimacy With God

Have you ever heard someone say, *"O, l want to know God. l want to be close to God"*? Intimacy with God is one of the New Covenant's benefits. We can access so much when we make Jesus Christ our Lord and Saviour. In fact, Paul put it this way: "the unsearchable riches of Christ" (Ephesians 3:8).

"For the wages of sin is death, but the [h]gift of God is eternal life in Christ Jesus our Lord" (Romans 6:23).

When we come to Christ, we have eternal life.

What is eternal life?

"And this is eternal life, that they may know You, the only true God, and Jesus Christ whom You have sent" (John 17:3).

We can see from the above scripture that eternal life is knowing the only true God and Jesus Christ He has sent.

"Eternal life means to know and experience you

as the only true God,

and to know and experience Jesus Christ,

as the Son whom you have sent" (John 17:3; TPT).

The Book of Hebrews also elaborates on this point:

"*10 For this is the covenant that I will make with the house of Israel after those days, saith the Lord; I will put my laws into their mind, and write them in their hearts: and I will be to them a God, and they shall be to me a people:*

11 And they shall not teach every man his neighbour, and every man his brother, saying, Know the Lord: ***for all shall know me, from the least to the greatest****"* (Hebrews 8:10-11; KJV).

As a believer in Christ, do you desire to know God more? The provision is already available under the New Covenant.

All we need to do is "draw near to Him" (James 4:8).

Diligently seek Him (Hebrews 11:6).

Peace With God

Did you know that you have peace with God? As believers, we can come boldly to the throne of Grace (Hebrews 4:16). We would only want to approach a person boldly when we know that we have peace with them.

"*Therefore, having been justified by faith, [a]****we have peace with God through our Lord Jesus Christ***" (Romans 5:1).

Jesus Christ is our peace.

"*14 For He Himself is our peace, who has made both one, and has broken down the middle wall of separation, 15 having abolished in His flesh the enmity, that is, the law of commandments contained in ordinances, so as to create in Himself one new man from the two, thus making peace*" (Ephesians 2:14-15).

Isn't it amazing that we have peace with the One who made heaven and earth? This is part of what Jesus Christ, our Lord, paid for—peace with God.

Living Through Jesus Christ

The Old Testament saints could not say, "I can do all things through Christ who strengthens me." Indeed, we do have a better covenant.

God sent Jesus Christ so that the world might be saved through Him.

"*16 For God so loved the world that He gave His only begotten Son, that whoever believes in Him should not perish but have everlasting life. 17 For God did not send His Son into the world to condemn the world, **but that the world through Him might be saved***" (John 3:16-17).

We are saved through Jesus Christ, and once saved, we live through Him:

"*9 In this the love of God was manifested toward us, that God has sent His only begotten Son into the world, that we **might live through Him***" (1 John 4:9).

We are not living this walk in our own strength. Therefore, we need to learn how to yield to the help we have been given.

So, what does that look like? Always ask the Lord for help. Always ask the Lord what to do, not what you want to do. Let's cast our cares upon the Lord. The Lord is interested in every minute of our lives.

Seated with Him in Heavenly Places

The Old Testament saints could not say, *"God has raised us up, and now we are seated together with Christ in heavenly places"*.

Why?

Because Jesus Christ, our Lord, had not yet paid the price for mankind.

Everything Jesus did was for us and is part of the benefits of the New Covenant.

"⁴ But God, who is rich in mercy, for his great love wherewith he loved us,

⁵ Even when we were dead in sins, hath quickened us together with Christ, (by grace ye are saved;)

⁶ And hath raised us up together, and made us sit together in heavenly places in Christ Jesus" (Ephesians 2:4-6; KJV).

We need to meditate on this spiritual reality. It is a place of authority in Christ. I would advise you to do additional research on this spiritual reality. Jesus Christ, our Lord, has given the church authority under this New Covenant.

Sons of God

Under the New Covenant, we are sons of God. In the Old Testament, some who walked with God were called servants or friends of God but not sons of God.

"*¹⁰ He was in the world, and the world was made by him, and the world knew him not.*

¹¹ He came unto his own, and his own received him not.

¹² But as many as received him, to them gave he power to become the sons of God, even to them that believe on his name" (John 1:10-12; KJV).

Another scripture reads:

"*Behold, what manner of love the Father hath bestowed upon us, that we should be called the sons of God: therefore the world knoweth us not, because it knew him not.*

² Beloved, now are we the sons of God, and it doth not yet appear what we shall be: but we know that, when he shall appear, we shall be like him; for we shall see him as he is" (1 John 3:1-2; KJV).

We are now sons of God, and we must meditate and study further on this. This is how we will be effective in this life.

As sons of God, we have the privilege of being led by the Spirit of God.

"For as many as are led by the Spirit of God, they are the sons of God" (Romans 8:14; KJV).

Authority to Use the Name of Jesus

In the Old Testament, the saints did not have the name of Jesus to use.

We are privileged to be given the name that is above every name. When did the name of Jesus become available to us?

"⁸ And being found in appearance as a man, He humbled Himself and became obedient to the point of death, even the death of the cross. ⁹ Therefore God also has highly exalted Him and given Him the name which is above every name, ¹⁰ that at the name of Jesus every knee should bow, of those in heaven, and of those on earth, and of those under the earth, ¹¹ and that every tongue should confess that Jesus Christ is Lord, to the glory of God the Father" (Philippians 2:8-11).

Therefore, every believer has a covenant right to use the name of Jesus:

*"¹⁷ And these signs will follow those who [d] believe: **In My name** they will cast out demons; they will speak with new tongues; ¹⁸ they[e] will take up serpents; and if they drink anything deadly, it will by no means hurt them; they will lay hands on the sick, and they will recover"* (Mark 16:17-18).

From the above, under the New Covenant, we can cast out demons, speak in new tongues, and enjoy other privileges in the name of Jesus.

We also have the authority to use the name of Jesus in prayer.

"¹³ And whatever you ask in My name, that I will do, that the Father may be glorified in the Son. ¹⁴ If you [c]ask anything in My name, I will do it" (John 14:13-14).

The Promise of the Holy Spirit

Under the Old Testament, before Jesus Christ, our Lord, paid the price for us, the Holy Spirit came upon men only for a specific purpose. Could this be why David prayed that the Lord not take His Holy Spirit from him (Psalm 51:11)?

Under the New Covenant, Jesus Christ promised He would give us another comforter that would be with us forever (John 14:26). We, as believers today, have the person of the Holy Spirit living with us for those that ask for Him. The indwelling of the Holy Spirit is a separate experience from the new birth (Acts 19:1-6). All we need to do is ask for Him as He is a gift (Luke 11:13).

The Holy Spirit guides us into all truth. He shows us things to come (John 16:13). He teaches us and brings all things to our remembrance (John 14:26). What an honour and privilege we have under the New Covenant!

The Holy Spirit also gives us gifts (1 Corinthians 12:4).

Led By the Spirit of God

Under the New Covenant, we are led by the Spirit of God (Romans 8:14). In the Old Testament, the people had to search for and seek prophets to know what God was saying because they did not have the person of the Holy Spirit abiding with them. Today, we can seek God ourselves and be led by His Spirit.

"*For as many as are led by the Spirit of God, they are the sons of God*" (Romans 8:14; KJV).

Life of God/Health

When Jesus Christ came, He came to give us life.

"*The thief does not come except to steal, and to kill, and to destroy. I have come that they may have life, and that they may have it more abundantly*" (John 10:10).

Everyone would agree that a prosperous life includes good health.

We have other scriptures that confirm further that Jesus came to take away sickness and disease.

"*Surely He has borne our [g]griefsAnd carried our [h]sorrows;Yet we [i]esteemed Him stricken,[j]Smitten by God, and afflicted.⁵ But He was wounded[k] for our transgressions,He was [l]bruised for our iniquities;The chastisement for our peace was upon Him,And by His stripes[m] we are healed*" (Isaiah 53:4-5).

Walking in divine health is part of our New Covenant.

"*Who his own self bare our sins in his own body on the tree, that we, being dead to sins, should live unto righteousness: by whose stripes ye were healed*" (1 Peter 2:24; KJV).

Prosperity

The Lord is not against us being rich; it is the love of money that the Bible speaks against (1 Timothy 6:10).

"For you know the grace of our Lord Jesus Christ, that though He was rich, yet for your sakes He became poor, that you through His poverty might become rich" (2 Corinthians 8:9).

"Beloved, I wish above all things that thou mayest prosper and be in health, even as thy soul prospereth" (3 John 2; KJV).

It is when we prosper that we can help others. It also takes money to proclaim the gospel.

God is not against us having abundance for the extension of His Kingdom.

Boldness to Come to the Throne of Grace

Because of the sacrifice of Jesus Christ, we can now come boldly unto the throne of grace.

"14 Seeing then that we have a great High Priest who has passed through the heavens, Jesus the Son of God, let us hold fast our confession. 15 For we do not have a High Priest who cannot sympathize with our weaknesses,

but was in all points tempted as we are, yet without sin. ¹⁶ Let us therefore come boldly to the throne of grace, that we may obtain mercy and find grace to help in time of need" (Hebrews 4:14-16).

We can always come boldly to the throne of grace to obtain mercy and find grace to help in times of need.

When we are struggling with anything or a situation, we can come boldly to the throne of grace to obtain mercy and find grace for help in times of need.

Christ Now Lives in Us

Under the New Covenant, Christ lives in us.

"I have been crucified with Christ; it is no longer I who live, but Christ lives in me; and the life which I now live in the flesh I live by faith in the Son of God, who loved me and gave Himself for me" (Galatians 2:20).

Living with the consciousness that Christ lives in us will have an impact our Christian walk and experience.

We Are the Temple of the Living God

"¹⁶ Do you not know that you are the temple of God and *that* the Spirit of God dwells in you?" (1 Corinthians 3:16).

Under the New Covenant, we are the temple of the living God.

These are just a few of our benefits under the New Covenant. As we have stated before, our God is a covenant-keeping God. We need to renew our minds with the truth of these realities.

Did you know that our covenant is an everlasting one?

"*20 Now may the God of peace who brought up our Lord Jesus from the dead, that great Shepherd of the sheep, **through the blood of the everlasting covenant**, 21 make you [a] complete in every good work to do His will, working in [b] you what is well pleasing in His sight, through Jesus Christ, to whom be glory forever and ever. Amen*" (Hebrews 13:20-21).

In the Old Testament, God told Moses to make the tabernacle according to the pattern he saw on the mount (Exodus 25:40). What Moses made was a shadow of heavenly things (Hebrews 8:5), and part of this was the Ark of the Covenant.

"*Then verily the first covenant had also ordinances of divine service, and a worldly sanctuary.*

2 For there was a tabernacle made; the first, wherein was the candlestick, and the table, and the shewbread; which is called the sanctuary.

3 And after the second veil, the tabernacle which is called the Holiest of all;

*4 Which had the golden censer, and the **ark of the covenant** overlaid round about with gold, wherein was the golden pot that had manna, and Aaron's rod that budded, and the tables of the covenant;*

A BETTER COVENANT

⁵ And over it the cherubims of glory shadowing the mercyseat; of which we cannot now speak particularly" (Hebrews 9:1-5; KJV).

We can find the description of the Ark of the Covenant in the Book of Exodus (Exodus 25:9-16). We now know this was in accordance with the heavenly pattern (Hebrews 8:5).

Just as Moses had the Old Covenant in an ark, did you know that our Covenant is actually a physical substance in heaven?

"Then the temple of God was opened in heaven, and the ark of [] His covenant was seen in His temple. And there were lightnings, noises, thunderings, an earthquake, and great hail" (Revelation 11:19).

Now that we know we have a better covenant, how will this become a physical reality in our lives?

Chapter Five

How to Implement the Benefits of the New Covenant

Now that we are aware of the benefits we have under the New Covenant, how do we implement them so that they become practical realities in our lives?

The first step is to come unto Jesus Christ and make Him Lord and Saviour of our lives.

We become partakers of the covenant by being translated into the Kingdom of Jesus Christ, our Lord (Colossians 1:13), and partakers of the covenants of promise (Ephesians 2:12).

A BETTER COVENANT

We then need to renew our minds in light of these spiritual realities.

This kingdom that we are now in works through faith.

The just shall live by faith (Romans 1:17); without faith, it is impossible to please God (Hebrews 11:6).

So, how do we assess what belongs to us? First, it is through faith and patience that we will inherit the promises (Hebrews 6:12).

Therefore, we need to know what belongs to us. Faith in what belongs to us in the New Covenant will come by hearing (Romans 10:17). It is the truth that will make us free (John 8:32). In this case, we are talking about the truth of us knowing the benefits we have in the New Covenant.

Once we come to Christ, the next step is coming to the knowledge of the truth. Yes, we must be born again; however, it does not stop there. We must come to the knowledge of the truth. This is God's will for us.

"Who will have all men to be saved, and to come unto the knowledge of the truth" (1 Timothy 2:4; KJV).

The knowledge of the truth includes the knowledge of the benefits of the New Covenant.

Coming to Christ has so many benefits, and when we know what we have, it makes our Christian experience more effective.

Let's now look at an example of accessing a benefit under the New Covenant. Intimacy with God is part of our inheritance in Christ. Eternal life is knowing God (John 17:3).

So, let's say a person wants to know God more and be closer to the Lord. The first step is to know that this is already available. We don't need to beg God; *O God, please, let me know who you are*. We are children of God.

Therefore, in such a case, we need to renew our minds to this truth and agree that God wants to fellowship with us as we do (1 John 1:3). We then need to put practical steps in place to draw closer to God. Read His word, spend time with the Lord, make right decisions, and do whatever the Holy Spirit instructs or guides us to do.

There are so many aspects of the covenant that we need a practical application to apply to our lives. The first point of all is that we must know what belongs to us and believe in it. The Bible says, "All things are possible to him that believes" (Mark 9:23).

Just as we found out that the Old Testament saints had their part to play, so do we have our own part to play. For example, despite God's promise to Abraham that his seed would have the land, some did not enter because of unbelief (Hebrews 3:19).

Therefore, another thing we need to address is our belief system. God has done His part, and we know that God keeps covenants. We need to know what belongs to us and the practical steps for it to become a reality in our lives.

The Bible says, "Fight the good fight of faith" (1 Timothy 6:12). Why is it called a good fight? Because we have already won. Jesus has already given us victory (2 Corinthians 2:14). The lack of knowledge can also hinder us from being partakers of what already belongs to us (Hosea 4:6).

God the Father loves us, and He wants the best for us.

Chapter Six

Conclusion

Isn't it great to know that our God keeps covenants? We've looked at some Old Covenants and see what our God did to ensure the security of His covenant. Abraham has gone many years, yet our God has not forgotten the covenant He made with him: *"In thee all the families of the earth shall be blessed"* (Genesis 12:3; KJV).

The Bible says we have a better covenant established on better promises (Hebrews 8:6).

We need to meditate and ensure that we know our covenant rights and how to implement them.

This book has introduced us to our better covenant. At least, we now know some of the benefits we have.

As we seek the face of the Lord, study His Word, and mature in Him, we will know better how to implement what already belongs to us!

Our God is faithful, and He is a covenant keeper.

About the Author

Bisi Oladipupo has been a Christian for many years and lives in the United Kingdom with her family.

Bisi attended a few Bible colleges, and she has completed a diploma in Biblical Studies from a UK Bible college.

She is a teacher of God's Word, coordinates Bible studies, and has a YouTube channel at https://www.youtube.com/c/BisiOladipupo123.

Her author page is www.bisiwriter.com

She writes regularly, and her blog website is www.inspiredwords.org

You can contact Bisi by email at bisiwriter@gmail.com

Books Also by Bisi

1. The Twelve Apostles of Jesus Christ: Lessons We Can Learn
2. The Lord's Cup in Communion: The Significance of taking the Lord's Supper
3. Different Ways to Receive Healing from Scripture and Walk in Health
4. Believing on The Name of Jesus Christ: What Every Believer Needs to Know
5. The Mind and Your Christian Walk: The Impact of the mind on our Christian walk
6. Relationship Skills in the Bible: Scriptural Principles of relating to others
7. The Nature of God's Kingdom: The Characteristics of the Kingdom of God
8. The Person of the Holy Spirit

A BETTER COVENANT

9. 41 Insights from the Book of Revelation

10. The Importance of Spiritual Discernment

11. God Speaks Through Nature

12. It's All About the Heart

Afterword

If you enjoyed this book, please take a few moments to write a review of it online at the store where it was purchased. Thank you!

Salvation Prayer

Father God, I come to you in Jesus' name. I admit that I am a sinner, and I now receive the sacrifice that Jesus Christ paid for me.

I confess with my mouth the Lord Jesus, and I believe in my heart that God raised Him from the dead.

I now declare that Jesus Christ is my Lord and Saviour.

Thank you, Father, for saving me in Jesus' name.

I am now your child. Amen.

If you've said this prayer for the first time, send an email to Bisiwriter@gmail.com . Start reading your Bible and ask the Lord to guide you to a good church.

www.ingramcontent.com/pod-product-compliance
Lightning Source LLC
Chambersburg PA
CBHW030045100526
44590CB00011B/334